Crossing the Chasm

Crossing the Chasm

A call to every Christian to love Muslim people

Kent Hodge

authorHOUSE®

AuthorHouse™ UK Ltd.
1663 Liberty Drive
Bloomington, IN 47403 USA
www.authorhouse.co.uk
Phone: 0800.197.4150

Published by AuthorHouse 11/21/2013

ISBN: 978-1-4918-8442-3 (sc)
ISBN: 978-1-4918-8443-0 (e)

Front and back cover design by John Hodge.

This book is printed on acid-free paper.

Printed in Great Britain by Clays Ltd, St Ives plc

With thanks to Ruth Hodge and Helen Blake (lftn.net) for their work and suggestions in editing this booklet. With appreciation for all our dear friends who encouraged us in the writing of this booklet and to all who pray for and support Christian Faith Ministries. With thanks also to many others whose ideas and ministries contributed to this booklet.

Praying along with you for wonderful local and global renewal:

"Your Kingdom come. Your will be done on earth as it is in heaven."

Our Mission to Muslims

It's not yet 7am here at Christian Faith Institute in Jos, Northern Nigeria and many of the 400 or so students are already in class. Student chapels are in progress and the sounds of preaching in French, Hausa and English can be heard in different sections of the college. Anyone listening would think each student was preaching to a crowd of a million people, challenging any opposition daring to withstand God's power!

The men and women here are exuberant, and a strong sense of fellowship, of purposeful mission and fulfillment permeates the college. Every day these people defy unimaginable obstacles to the spread of the gospel: Islamic fundamentalist terrorist groups bombing churches, schools and moderate mosques; targeted assassinations of pastors and their families; Christian homes set on fire while the family is sleeping, men carrying AK47's ready to shoot anyone trying to escape; murder of teachers, nurses and other community leaders; ethnic conflict destroying whole villages or suburbs. All of this is in addition to the general poverty, too few and poorly equipped, expensive hospitals and schools, and a desperate lack of infrastructure. Even so, the gospel is breaking through. Revival is spreading through this part of Africa and sweeping all before it. The inimitable gospel prevails because it alone is the liberating truth.

For 20 years my wife Ruth and I worked with the ministry of Archbishop Benson Idahosa in Southern Nigeria. In his time 30 million people came into churches in the nation, mainly in the witchcraft-dominated south. In those years I would walk down the hall to Benson's office, gazing at the photos of evangelistic crusades he had conducted with up to one million people in attendance. Crutches and wheelchairs were held above the crowd in rejoicing at the miracles God did. I would think: "What about the north? What about Islam? What about the future?"

Those years prepared us for the battle being fought now in the Muslim dominated north of Nigeria. As we grew we took on more responsibility as the leaders of the All Nations For Christ Bible Institute Benson had founded. 8,000 pastors passed through training in our years there, most of whom were sponsored by our friends and family in Australia. They have planted thousands of churches all over the world. Ruth and I often faced overwhelming situations and on a few occasions I shared them with Benson. Each time he simply said, "God will do it." Leaving his office, I would know God would do it. Benson's faith filled me with a deep confidence. And of course, God did do it, every time.

Benson was a real father in the Lord to us. He didn't say, "Well, you have just taken on too much. What were you thinking?" He stood with us. Now, God has called us to be father and mother to so many others who need nurturing.

In the late 1980's, before the Soviet Union collapsed, Benson was being interviewed by the press in the UK. He told them boldly that Communism was about to collapse and the region would open wide to the gospel. That's exactly what happened, soon afterwards when the Berlin wall came down. The UK press wanted to hear more, so later they asked him what would happen next. He answered, "Islam is coming down." As with the Berlin wall's collapse, God's intervention in the Muslim world will have wider impact. All of the Muslim populations of Europe and Muslim migrants in Western nations will be affected.

Benson resisted the overwhelming onslaught of Islam in his nation. Twice on national television he publically "rescinded" a presidential decree declaring Islam the national religion. Twice the decree was withdrawn.

What about us? Many of us complain about Islam. We can sit in our comfort face-booking our concerns. We think there is some kind of value in noticing what is wrong, but anyone can see what is wrong. It's responding with faith, doing something because of faith in the gospel that counts with God.

For many years Ruth and I have felt personally drawn to the Islamic peoples. We love them. God loves them. Here is where we need action. It's not just faith; it's also love, which is a verb, a "doing" word. When we have a heart of love for people, fear is overcome. When we put people first, our fears will eventually be resolved.

What Do We See?

Many years ago, God drew Ruth and me to the story in Genesis 21 where Ishmael was dying in the desert. A well of water was there, but neither Ishmael nor his mother Hagar saw it. When God opened Hagar's eyes she saw the well. Spiritually, those in Islam today draw from this Ishmael heritage. The well of water, Jesus Christ, has been among them for a long time, but many of them haven't seen him. The eyes of our understanding can see from this story that God loves the Islamic peoples and is able to open their eyes *en masse* to the Son of God. They will drink the waters of life and be revived in the desert. God wants us to see that the harvest is ripe already (John 4:35). Can we see this? Can we believe it? Do we have faith to believe this?

The enemy believes it and is in a rage trying to prevent it. Just as Herod slew the children when Christ was born, today's terrorists, inspired by the same enemy, are using similar tactics to try to stop the Son of God. Herod created terror but did not succeed. The enemy believes in the harvest that is coming in the Muslim world and with fury he is trying to prevent it. But God has already gone before us and prepared the way. The enemy is using his last card, before the gates are opened and the gospel comes like a flood into the Islamic nations.

We can respond either with fear or with faith. We can look at what is against the church or we can look at the One who is with the church. Countless examples in the Old Testament tell of God's people being up against impossible opposition. Each one of these occasions became their finest hour: Gideon broke through with a small number; Elisha saw that those who are for us are more than those against us; Hezekiah led a nation-sweeping revival when the greatest army of his day was camped outside the walls. It's a matter of what we put our trust in. Do we trust in the Lord?

We can't serve God when we are serving ourselves. We can only serve when we trust the Lord with our lives. "They overcame him by the blood of the Lamb, by the word of their testimony (the gospel), and by not loving their own lives, even to death." (Rev 12:11)

Now is not the time to be on the defensive and in retreat. It's time to be on the front foot with the power of the gospel. Only God has the answers people need and are looking for in their lives. Only the gospel of Jesus Christ reveals the answers. We have this gospel. We are unique. The more the enemies of God come out against the church, the more the power of the gospel shines. The greater the darkness, the more clearly the light is seen. So, what are we afraid of? The greatest hour of the church is ahead of us! "When the enemy comes in like a flood, the Spirit of the Lord will raise up a standard against him." (Isaiah 59:19)

Our fear is really about the fear of loss: "What will happen to me?" This holds us back. It held people back in Gideon's time, when the Hebrews also had the Creator of the world with them. It's a matter of perception, what we are looking at. Are we seeing the power of the enemy? Or are we seeing the power of God? Angels are all around us, and yet we often don't see that the God we serve is with us. Let's not react by fear. Fear creates a negative mindset. We close our doors, shutting out a world of people in need. Fear paralyses, but the gospel is dynamic power, breaking through all opposition.

Can we see that God rules our nations and the movement of populations today? Why else would Satan inspire terror if he weren't so afraid of the power in the gospel? Can we see how much he believes in the power of the gospel? He knows that when the gospel is declared freely in the Middle

East it will smash open the bondage he has worked so long to cultivate by holding people in darkness. It's time we believed this!

Right now, more Muslims in Egypt are coming to Christ than ever before in the history of the nation. Nearby in Turkey the internet is opening up millions of people to hear the gospel. A young Australian man we know travelled through Iran as a tourist with a snowboard, praying with Iranians of all ages. Almost without exception, the Iranian people were open and hungry to hear about Jesus. All over the Middle Eastern region young people are secretly using Christian websites via mobile phone apps, studying Christian discipleship courses. Mothers and grandmothers watch satellite Christian broadcasts and text in more questions than the follow-up workers can cope with. "The harvest is ALREADY ripe, but the labourers are few."

In Nigeria's north right now, the eyes of great numbers of Muslims are being opened to Jesus by dreams and visions. In Jos at the Christian Faith Institute, we have ex-terrorists and ex-radical extremists studying for ministry, planting churches and reaching hundreds of thousands with the gospel. Almost half of our students are believers from a Muslim background. Some are being sheltered in the college from Sharia law death sentences. Others have come to us after going through a period of discipleship in safe houses. They come for training answering the call to reach their own Islamic people groups. One student's mother saw Jesus at Mecca when she was on holy pilgrimage, and was born again right there. There are so many examples we could share of how Jesus is opening eyes, just like he did for Hagar. He is impacting hearts, changing lives and destinies forever.

Among the refugees currently coming to Australia are many Iranians, fleeing from Iran for various reasons. Some come because they belong to an Islamic sect whose followers are persecuted in Iran; others are Christian; others are enemies of the Iranian government. In Melbourne there is a revival happening among Iranian Muslims. Churches are baptizing them into Jesus Christ. The church is embracing and loving these people, getting out of their comfort zones and preaching the gospel to them. How wrong it would be to prevent them from coming into our country when here the gospel is free to spread if we will spread it.

The fear of Islam or fearing Muslim people coming into our Western nations by immigration is not a right response. We shouldn't be intimidated by their faces, by their different culture, or customs. Don't be deceived by intimidation. They are people who need the same love and faith we have. We need to show them the love of God, to believe in the power of the gospel more than in the darkness of bondage. Let's follow Jesus' way. Let's realize that their coming to our country, even if with an Islamic agenda, is God's plan to open their countries up to him. We focus so much on the enemy's plans, but can we see God's plan? God gave us the Great Commission, to reach all nations with the gospel. Now the nations are coming to us. They are coming to where we have the liberty to reach them. We cannot retreat from the clear commission of Jesus: "Go into all nations (every people group) and preach this gospel to every person."

Today is the day for the church to explode through the nations in power. God has promised it. Jesus is the heir of the world. "The abundance of the sea (gentile peoples) shall be converted to him." "He shall be king over all the earth." "Through your seed I will bless all the families of the earth." "Why do the heathen rage and try to do a vain thing? God will laugh at them and put them into confusion . . ." "I have set my King upon my holy hill Zion (he rules now from God's right hand in heaven)." "He shall reign from sea to sea, from the river to the end of the world." "Sit at my right hand till I make your enemies your footstool." "All the ends of the world shall remember and turn to the Lord." How can any other conspiracy agenda prevail against what God has already promised and is currently bringing to pass through his church?

There will be opposition. When opposition comes it will not mean that our expectation was wrong, that we have been mistaken. It's not always easy to keep living God's way, but it becomes easy when we do it. That's when God takes over for us. There is a battle but God wins, so let's not be overwhelmed by the enemy's actions.

When Samaria was under Syrian siege, four despairing lepers took courage and moved in the right direction. That's all it took for things to become entirely different for them. (2 Kings 7) On the same day elsewhere in Samaria, the King's personal attendant was present when Elisha declared, "Listen to what the Lord says! By this time tomorrow in Samaria there will be an abundance of food. You will be able to buy ten pounds of the best wheat or twenty pounds of barley for one piece of silver." The personal attendant responded, "Even if the Lord himself were to open heaven's windows, I can't see how that could possibly happen." "You will see it happen," Elisha replied, "but you won't get to eat any of the food."

The fear of Islam among many Christians is based on a lie: that Islam is significant. But it is not significant when measured against the power of God. When we step forward in God the enemy camp hears a rumble. They hear the noise of a great army and flee the battle. God is mighty to save when all seems lost, after he has brought us, his people, to repentance for our lack of faith in him.

May Your Kingdom Come

Around the world today there is a cultural divide between "conservatives" and "liberals". Conservatism often claims to be following biblical values, but like the pharisaic stance it can miss the whole point of the law: love for God, for our neighbour, the sinner and the foreigner. Jesus' teaching and life-style demonstrated that he was probably more opposed to "conservatism", as modeled by the Pharisees, than he was opposed to anything else. Jesus sought out sinners, and did not condemn them. He identified with them and shared in their reproach from the religious people. He did all he possibly could to show that he identified with and loved them, even dying the death of a criminal. On the other hand, liberalism casts doubt on biblical authenticity. The danger of liberalism is compromising truth. Compromise can be a corrupting leaven in society. As Christians we have a zeal for truth and are jealous to guard biblical values. We want to see his truth prevailing in our communities, setting people free, honoring God and remolding our societies.

Neither conservatism nor liberalism is biblically correct. Both have hijacked the Christian message. As followers of Jesus we are called to a *truth position*. We are called to think as God thinks, as revealed in scripture. This includes a *love posture*, to reach out sacrificially to sinners and to accept the suffering just as Jesus did. This is following the spirit of Jesus. We agree our societies need to be renewed by God's truth, but how is this achieved? It begins with the spirit in which we operate. God's truth must be established God's way by the spirit of Jesus, or it isn't his kingdom that's being established.

Conservatism is too often more about protecting our life style than protecting the honour of God. It can be an alluring message. For example, we might attend a meeting that informs us about the global Islamic agenda. The facts presented might be true but the listeners will more than likely leave the meeting with a wall-building mentality of resistance to Muslim people. Most listeners would not go away from such a meeting with the spirit Jesus had when he said he "must go to Samaria", a place despised by Israel. To be educated about the truths of Islam is good, but it only goes a part of the distance. Jesus calls us to go all the way.

Conservatism is alluring because it fits our Western middle class isolation. We aren't drawn to love and reach our enemy with the gospel. Rather than attend meetings furnishing us with skills in intra-community bridge building we are more likely to attend one that will strengthen the walls and encourage replenishing the moat with crocodiles.

We might argue, "If we don't build walls, our life style is at risk." That might be true, but was this the message of Jesus? He spoke of losing our life as being the way to find it. He spoke of loving our enemy, of building his kingdom, not saving ours. His kingdom is built with bridges and self-giving, which he modeled for us. Our kingdoms are too often built with walls and guns.

The incarnation of the Son of God was the greatest bridge to enemies ever built. God calls us to do the same. His kingdom is "not of this world", but throughout church history we have confused and blended our kingdoms with his. The apostle James said Christ's kingdom is about the way we treat others: "the royal law". If we had paid heed to James throughout church history, many of the things done in Jesus' name would never have been done. Christendom was burning synagogues, killing pagans and taxing unbelievers well before Muhammad followed the example. Today our economic imperialism and warfare industry are very inconsiderate of the suffering of so many people. It's not a matter of who is more righteous in all this. We are to learn to treat all others with the same grace our Lord Jesus Christ has extended to us.

People respond when we treat them kindly. The battle for people and their souls is against Satan. Our desire is to win sinners and see God transform them. We win them by being a refuge, a storm shelter, where truth and grace meet together. We need to start seeing people as people who need the love of God like we do, not as the enemy. The answer isn't found by focusing on what the enemy is doing, but by seeing what God is doing through the gospel, setting people free from whatever it is that binds them.

The life, death and resurrection of Jesus are our model. "Let this mind be in you that was in Christ." (Phil 2:5) He didn't cling to his life. Reaching us was in his mind. We were evil, wicked and violent and killed him, yet he loved us and prayed, "Father, forgive them for they do not know what they are doing." Are we his followers? Are we doing for others who are evil, what he did for us when we were evil? Christ's resurrection shows that even if we die serving the enemy, the world will not be lost to an evil religion. It is fear to think it will be. God's Spirit will always change hearts and build Christ's kingdom, among all people on earth. No power is greater. God has promised it. Will God allow his kingdom to fail? Does he need us to build his kingdom our way? Aren't his promises good and faithful? Jesus trusted they were when he went to the cross.

The cross was Jesus' only strategy. It must also be ours, if we are his followers. Jesus went to the cross with this promise: "He shall see his seed (great numbers of spiritual offspring in all nations). God shall prolong his days (raise him from the dead). The pleasure of the Lord shall prosper in his hand." (Isaiah 53:10) This is also our promise today. There is no way that God's kingdom will not flourish in the entire world.

Christians young and old today need a vision for the future built on service and self-giving. These are the most motivating values. Our complaints about the state of things, our hatred of those who oppose the truth, our self-saving stance and preoccupation with end-times doomsday scenarios give no hope for the future and are de-motivating. Where are the hope, love and faith, which are at the centre of Jesus' nature? This is what we all need, what is worth living for.

We need a new vision of how Jesus lived towards his enemies and how this transformed them and the nations. This kind of living is the hope of our nations today. The church needs a new call back to this kind of discipleship.

Mercy for Others

The Pharisees thought they were right with God while they were shut off from sinners and from the suffering of a world in need. Conservatism gives us the false comfort that we are in right standing with God because we hold to the right doctrines, and have the light to make assessments on what is wrong in the world and about the sin of others. This was the stance of the Pharisees and something Jesus consistently condemned.

Luke tells us that Jesus gave a parable "for those who think they are right with God while despising those who are wrong." (Luke 18:9) These are biting words if we let them apply to ourselves. Jesus told of a Pharisee who went to the temple and prayed: "*I belong to the right group. I believe the right things.*" A tax collector came in to the temple and prayed as well: "*I am a stranger here, a sinner, not a member of this group.*" The tax collector didn't know the word of God, but God was able to touch his heart anyway. He beat his breast and cried, "God have mercy upon me a sinner."

Jesus said that this man, not the other man, was right before God.

The person we despise, the person we rally against, thinking we are doing the will of God, may in the end be the one who is right with God. He can touch the heart of any person anywhere in the world at any time. "With God all things are possible." We might do better to beat our own breast than to despise others. We can be right while completely missing the spirit of Jesus. Our dear friend, and Provost of our college in Jos, Emmanuel Razack, was brought up a Muslim. His father served as the Imam of their mosque for 60 years and strongly opposed the gospel. One morning last year Emmanuel's father renounced his Islamic prayers, confessed Christ and started studying the Bible. Two weeks later he died and went to be with the Lord.

In another parable, Jesus spoke of a Samaritan who helped an injured and destitute man on the road to Jericho. Other men, religious Jews, had passed by but hadn't stopped to help. They hadn't cared for their neighbour. Maybe they thought he wasn't part of their group. It was inconvenient, and the risk involved was too great. But the Samaritan, the despised enemy, the one of the wrong faith, showed instead, by his works, that he understood and knew God.

It was the one outside "the church" who showed the spirit of Jesus towards his enemy.

Having the right religious affiliation doesn't mean we know God, nor does it allow us to despise others. It is doing what the Samaritan did that shows we know God. As James said, "One will say to you: 'Show me your faith without your works and I will show you my faith by my works.'" Jesus taught that his kingdom isn't expressed by dotting all the conservative i's, but by extending his grace to others no matter what faith they come from. Jesus was clearly showing that all humanity are in brotherhood and are to be treated with equal love and care. The Prophets showed the same, "But let justice roll down like waters and righteousness like an ever-flowing stream." (Amos 5:24, Is 58, Jer 22:16) Christ came as the answer to Cain's question, "Am I my brother's keeper?"

In the story of Lazarus at the rich man's gate, the rich man had Moses' word and the words of the Prophets, yet he did not help Lazarus. Lazarus, an unimportant beggar, was the one who ended up in Abraham's bosom. Jesus said, "Many shall come from the east and from the west and sit down in the kingdom, while you shall be cast out." His listeners were constantly shocked by his teaching. "But we are the people of God, we are Israel!" They thought God's salvation was by the right affiliation, but it was not. Many outside Israel were forgiven and accepted by God. Moses' father-in-law acknowledged and respected God; Job (a non-Israelite) knew God; the Assyrians repented and were forgiven because of Jonah's preaching, without circumcision and without joining the temple.

Cornelius was a Centurion in the Roman army. The scriptures describe him as a devout man who feared God, prayed always and helped those in need. He was doing the will of God, not just believing something about God. God is looking for godliness that shows love and care toward others as he has loved us in Christ. Salvation came to Cornelius and all in his household. "Then Peter began to speak: "I now realize how true it is that God does not show favoritism, but he accepts from every nation the one who fears him and does what is right." (Acts 10:34-35) We might think Muslim people are the enemy, but there are many among them who live more godly lives than some of us.

Jonah had no care for his enemies. He was angry that God would love them and accept them. He had no compassion for the people, whereas God even cared for their animals: "And should I not have concern for the great city of Nineveh, in which there are more than a hundred and twenty thousand people who cannot tell their right hand from their left—and also many animals?" (Jonah 4:11)

We shouldn't be proud of our light, our knowledge, or affiliation. We should be humble and instead of pointing a finger to accuse, stretch out both of our hands to serve. This is what Christ did. This is what he taught in all of his parables. This is probably why the Jews did not like him. They thought he had come to deal with the enemy, to deal with Rome. Instead he has come that we should serve our enemies. This service is the nature of his kingdom which renews the world. The mark of faith is that we do what Jesus did, serve our enemies. This spirit of Jesus in our lives is the position from which the gospel is shared.

We need to be more involved in serving the world than withdrawing from it, more involved in the suffering of those of other faiths than in pointing the finger. Some will kill us, but we bear Christ, who gives the power to forgive and to serve, as well as to rise with him. When this service is what they see, many believe. We preach the gospel and we show the gospel by sharing his love with all, not just with our own. This is what Jesus was speaking about. Solomon secured his throne by killing his enemies. Who did Jesus kill to secure his eternal throne? Rather, he gave himself. We have no right, as followers of Christ, to depart from this.

"Then she wiped (Jesus' feet) with her hair, kissed them and poured perfume on them. When the Pharisee who had invited him saw this, he said to himself, 'If this man was a prophet, he would know who is touching him and what kind of woman she is, that she is a sinner.'" (Luke 7:38-39) The very people we are trying to keep away are the ones God is inviting into his kingdom. The very ones we exclude from our nation, our homes and churches are the ones God is calling. "Then Jesus added, "Now go and learn the meaning of this Scripture: 'I want you to show mercy, not offer sacrifices.' For I have come not to call those who think that they are righteous, but those who know they are sinners." (Matt 9:13)

A New View of the Church

We need a renewed view of the church. We have had a Western view, a church in many ways attached to Western culture and to our social traditions. We feel that if we open our doors to others too wide we will lose this. We forget that today the strongest growing Christian populations are in countries like India and China and in parts of Africa and South America. Western culture is not the equivalent of Christianity, despite the many benefits from its Christian heritage.

Jerusalem's Pharisees wanted a racial and social purity. They wanted to be in charge. Jesus' view of his church is very different from this type of mentality. He upset the Pharisees by making his headquarters in "Galilee of the Nations", a racially mixed region. This is where he chose to launch his kingdom, giving a clear message in his choice.

The future holds great hope of our moving out of our past "European Empire" style and concept of church into a church truly "of the nations" where we are ethnically mixed and learn each other's ways and grow to love each other in Christ. What we will gain is immense and rich in fellowship, far more than what we have known in the past. It will not be easy to get there and many will oppose it, but this new church will look a lot more like the church Jesus would build.

As the world's nations move closer together today with technology and travel, so much will be gained if we declare God's vision in Christ to our world. The next 100 years could so radically change and bless the world as the church moves onto the right foot and loves and serves all people in our local and wider communities.

We may fear "globalization conspiracies" that urge us to shun change, maintain the status quo and keep ourselves separate from the suffering. No doubt many have their conspiracy plans, but we believe in a greater plan, a greater "conspiracy" which is an open fact. God has already given the global future to Christ. "Ask of me and I will give you the nations for your inheritance, the uttermost part of the world for your possession." He makes all land his holy land through the reign of his King, extending the Old Testament promises and boundaries to the whole world. "The kingdoms of this world are becoming the kingdoms of the Lord and of his Christ."

We shouldn't fear as the Pharisees feared. We should open up and help people in need. We should reach out to and help people in the nations of the world as Israel was called to do and as Jesus commissioned the church to do. Instead of fearing what might happen to us, we must lose our life and believe what the love of Christ will do for others. The bottom line is that we are called to show love to others. Conservatism may make excuses not to, but Jesus compels us to shun excuses, and not to shun people in need.

As a young boy growing up in Sydney, I was bullied at school for having what people in those days derogatively referred to as a "WOG" friend (a friend from Italy). I didn't mind, because my friend's father cooked good fish and chips for us! Now, the social 'phobias' are against Middle Easterners, Muslims, sinners or those of different classes. We really need to change, to open up and to see people as Christ sees them. Then, our churches will begin to look more like Jesus' mission: "Go out into the highways and byways and compel them ALL to come in." The separation of nations at the Tower of Babel has been overcome by Christ and Pentecost. We now live in a new world, where Christ's kingdom is breaking through in people's hearts.

We need the right view of the church from scripture. It isn't all about an escape to heaven. It's God's plan to renew and bless the nations. God made Adam and Eve in his image and commissioned them to reflect this nature throughout the world. He renewed this commission through Israel who had God's Spirit and presence dwelling amongst them. For so long we have misread the main point of scripture, as being our personal justification for heaven, but it is about us being his image-bearers to the world, serving and renewing the world, which he redeemed on the cross.

"This is a house of prayer for all nations" (Mark 11:17) refers to the old temple, now the church, a living temple of people of all ethnicities and cultures. God has made us an elected people, a special priesthood because he loves the world, so we may show his love and care to all humankind. God forbid that we stay nationalistic or tribalistic as Israel did. We are one people in Christ, of all nations. Let's live this way, not just in fellowship with people like ourselves, but with all. It starts with us, actively reaching out to others, as Jesus actively came and reached out to us. Don't wait.

Miracle in Jos

In recent years and months Jos has experienced severe attacks against Christians. Thousands have been killed. Our suburb has been engulfed in violence with barely a building unscarred by bullet holes or untouched by fire. Many people have suffered loss of family. Many have lost their businesses, personal property and trade goods and may never recover them: there is no insurance or compensation. Villages close to our college were attacked one night and hundreds of people were massacred while we slept. Repeated attacks on ethnic "Christian" villages in the region by men armed with AK47s and grenade launchers have killed many and thousands have been driven in terror from their homes and farmland. Churches have been bombed during service times. Students from our college and friends, including bishops we have trained who stood to care for their churches, have been gunned down, murdered.

The situation became desperately bad. Increasing in intensity and frequency, skirmishes were not just about religion, but also politics and ethnic-cleansing issues occurring all over Nigeria. People divided into an ever increasing number of ethnic or ideological camps. It looked out of control, as if we were heading towards a national blood bath. But in the midst of this are so many people who love Jesus with all their hearts, with so much grace and salvation poured out on the churches.

The churches prayed. After years of preaching forgiveness and care for the enemy a miracle took everyone by surprise.

The army had moved into three north-eastern states and begun major operations against Boko Haram, the terrorist group that has led the attacks with strong international backing. We and others were urging fairness in the army's use of disciplinary force, care for the communities involved, righteous treatment of those in the region, and the use of resources to build a future for their people. An abrupt change of heart came to communities in the three states. The Muslims and Christians began to cooperate. Unarmed Muslim youth frequently stood between terrorists and Christians to protect them with their own lives. We heard a Muslim governor on the radio sincerely praising God for the gracious and undeserved outcome.

Community cooperation started all over the north of the nation. People began to talk about their problems with each other instead of killing. The number of sporadic killings has reduced drastically. In our city Jos, where we have such a diversity of racial and religious groups living together, representatives began meeting for talks that became meaningful. The people of the community spoke with one voice, saying they wanted the killings to stop. They wanted to live together in peace, rather than have a winner-takes-all attitude. "We can only win together", people began to say.

A student in one of my classes is a special advisor to the governor of our state. He sits on committees responsible for security and brings people together from different cultural backgrounds. He visits mosques. This can be hard when there has been so much danger and animosity. Friends, family or colleagues may have been murdered by people from the same mosques. But he and groups of other Christians are going to mosques and are being invited to sing Christian songs, pray Christian prayers and share the gospel. It is not a trap; there is no hidden motive. Most Muslims, like most Christians, want the violence to end. In my class he said he was shocked: "I haven't heard about this love before. They burnt my houses, so I burnt their houses and did terrible things." He is now speaking boldly on state media of Jesus and of one peaceful community for Jos.

Another CFI student took my book ~~Changing the World~~, *Changing Ourselves* to his besieged city of Maiduguri. His wife and other Christian leaders decided "the whole community must hear this message". They organized a meeting and 200 leaders from the Islamic Deputy Governor and Emir's offices, Imams and Islamic youth groups attended. The Sheik (leading Islamic scholar) of Maiduguri attended. Boko Haram "generals" came and spoke of churches they had bombed. Pastors came. At the meeting they taught from my book on the nature of God's kingdom and why Jesus came. The Muslims apologized for their killing and the pastors apologized for retaliation, for hating and shunning the Islamic community. They all agreed "we have all gone against the teachings and model of Jesus Christ" and the Muslim leaders said "we want to hear more of this Christ."

In situations like this Jesus becomes the standard bearer. He is utterly unique in history. He is the only one who came as Lord and who served all by giving his life and rising from the dead. He is the only one without sin, but who shows complete mercy. It is when we are willing to repent of our pride as Christians that Jesus is lifted up and becomes the banner for all others to see and rally to. It is so easy to point to Jesus in this way. Everybody in the Islamic community starts talking about Jesus: "Who is this Jesus?" They are used to hearing of the Jesus of the Crusades, where his people respond like everyone else, according to our own self-interest. When the pastors said, "forgive us", they answered, "We have never heard of *this* Christ before! We must hear more."

Recently a student stood in class and said, "I was a Muslim. I was persecuted so much when I became a Christian. I forgave them, but I would have nothing to do with them." This so describes many of our Christian lives. In tears he said he realised this isn't forgiveness. He has now opened his heart to his people and found ways of serving them. He is a carpenter so he began fixing some of their houses. Many of them began turning their lives over to Jesus. The student said the Muslim people in Kafanchan are easier to turn to Christ's love than the Christians. The Muslim Chief Security Officer, involved in so much killing before, is now texting our student every day to ask him about the ways of Christ. In an unprecedented move he gathered Muslim and Christian leaders together and asked our student to preach to them about Jesus' salvation. Now this Muslim leader is distributing this book *Crossing the Chasm* among the Muslims of his community.

Recently one of our staff and dear friends went to a Muslim home to celebrate *Eid al-Fitr*, deep inside the Islamic sector of our city, a very dangerous place for Christians. He then invited all the Islamic leaders of our community to my office to talk together. As we spoke I shared how we want to serve the community and we don't care what faith people are, we just want to treat people as people and help where there are needs. (There is so much need in all our communities and so much we can do.) As we discussed further we asked what they thought about us training their Islamic youth in computer skills, working inside the Islamic sector, where Christians normally never visit. Despite the terrorism in the nation aimed specifically at such education, the leaders were deeply touched and very grateful. We are now working together seeking to help thousands of Muslim youth have a future. They were shocked and asked, "With all the violence in this community, why are you doing this?" We answered this is what Jesus did for us when we were his enemies. It's so simple.

Thousands of Muslims in every district are coming to Jesus. We could go through testimony after testimony of what our students and graduates are seeing God do. So many Muslims are seeing Jesus in visions and miracles, or studying him in the Quran and then the Scriptures.

So many thousands of Muslims are coming to Christ in our own mission stations and in missions run by many of our friends. There is so much good happening because the biblical/Jesus' way we are to respond to our persecution is so easy for all to understand. When you love people during severe persecution they will eventually know your Jesus is real and come to him asking for grace and renewal. (Rev 3:9)

Peacemaking: Refusing
a Camp Mentality

As God's children one of the most important roles we have is to be peacemakers. "Blessed are the peacemakers, for they shall be called the children of God." (Matt 5:9) Peacemakers resemble God, who through the incarnation of Christ built a bridge to us when we were his enemies. This means we are to build bridges to those who are our enemies and seek to reach them with the love of God. When we experience division because of Christ our response must be like Christ's response to us: love for our enemies, forgiveness, actively seeking connections and communication with all people and living a self-denying peacemaking life-style. This is the call to every person who bears Christ.

A tendency of the church is to withdraw from society and separate ourselves into a camp against our enemies. We draw up our bridge and throw shots at the other camps. This leads to isolation. The subsequent lack of communication and lack of care for others is wrong, and dangerous to society. This isn't what Jesus did when he came. He always went to the enemy and ate and drank with them. He engaged them. He had no camp or drawbridge mentality. Jesus said that there would be opposition to the gospel, but that our response should be to follow his model of non-violent and selfless outreach. His task for us is to be healers in Christ's tradition, in his footsteps.

The early church did not cut itself off. The believers persisted at the synagogues, at the temple and the Jewish feasts. They knew that Christ had fulfilled these feasts and that they were free of obligation to them, but they reached out to their Jewish neighbours at risk of death. Although the Jews rejected them angrily, the church kept coming back, appealing to them with eager tenderness: "Abraham *our* father . . ." Where is this kind of charity today? We have been so careful to deny any common links with Muslims. The early church could equally have done this with the Jews (John 8:39, Rom 2:28-29, 9:8, Gal 3:7), but instead they loved them intensely, respected the common godliness and were "all things to all men that they may save some."

Yes, others who are different are our brothers in many ways, and this should be respected, just as the early church respected it. But we strongly desire that they may also be brothers in Christ. It is the work of the Holy Spirit to turn their hearts to Christ as we engage and interact with them. We have become such keen separatists that we no longer recognize or have the skills for community brotherhood with others who are different. We are not one faith with Muslims, but we are one community in our societies. We must learn to love them this way and do something about it.

One of our Bible College students at Christian Faith Institute, a Fulani, reaches thousands of Fulani people in the bush. (The Fulani are an aggressively Islamic, nomadic people group). He says that if Jesus were here today he would go to the mosques, because he came for the sinner. Most of us wouldn't dare attend a mosque. We prefer to stay in our own circles. But grace connects to the things we have in common to show us Christ. That is how Christ won us. Jesus came as a Jew to the Jews and came to us in our culture.

When we speak against Muslims it is often from a desire to justify our separation, to excuse our lack of engagement. Jesus will not honour this when we meet him. There are things that we have in common with Muslims: a fear of God is in many of their hearts through common grace. Peacemaking means we reach across the chasm and build a bridge to them. It means we are inclusive of them. We don't have to disrespect them, or pull down the genuine part of their godliness many may have inherited from their Jewish and Christian past. We can appeal to it in love and this will reveal Jesus.

The miracle that is happening in Jos testifies to how dramatically things can change when we live Jesus' way. I am not saying that the problems are all over, but I am saying there is a right way for Christians to walk, to be involved with others in society and not to be aloof from them. There is a way for the Christian to lead, a demonstration of the reconciliation we preach. It is pointless preaching a gospel we don't also live. Walking Jesus' way is *leading* the kingdom way. It will cost us something; that is why Jesus put the cross at the centre of all he taught. None of this can work without the cross.

We are not being naïve; not saying that no one has evil intent, that there are no Islamic plots and that there won't be more killing. There are many potentially destructive cultural, political, social and religious obstacles ahead. So, we need to pray always, knowing that nations and people act in their own self-interest and not for the common good. We all do this. We can never take things for granted, but are called to vigilance. But, our vigilance isn't against a culture or a people, but against the common enemy we all have. Our tactics against this enemy are different: they are love and outreach, rather than apathy and self-centeredness. Rather than studying the nature of Islamic plots and responding in the flesh, we study the life and nature of Jesus to determine our response. We are saying, "Don't become like our enemy." "Overcome evil with good."

Peace-making has opened a wide door for evangelism in our region in Jos and beyond, to millions of precious souls. Outreach is intensifying and many are coming to know Jesus. Within our Western nations we must also take the initiative. We must follow Jesus in reaching across cultural borders and camps, getting to know and learning to love others. We must learn to be one community with all people in our societies, with all races, backgrounds and faiths, so the love of Jesus may freely spread among all people. This will in time open doors to millions of souls, just as it did in the book of Acts. This is Jesus' way. We can't be content to live our own lives when Christ gave his life for all. "He is the propitiation for our sins, but not for ours only, but also for the whole world." (1 John 2:2)

Reaching Across the Chasm

Our societies have become multicultural. For those who wish it were otherwise, there is no way for the time to be turned back. What we need to do is see the way things are with eyes of faith based in God's love for all people, not fear.

In our societies we are to be part of the larger community. The love we Christians learn together is to be shared with others. We need to seek cooperation with people of other faiths and racial backgrounds with whom we share society. They are more similar to us than we believe.

We haven't realized that "rejoice with those who rejoice and weep with those who weep" doesn't only mean among friends or fellow-believers. Our religious celebrations and feasts are a good example. Instead of only going to our own (Easter, Christmas), we should accept sincere invitations to others' feasts and also invite them to ours. The attitude we have that someone's faith being wrong means we can't rejoice in their religious feasts, isn't right. It isn't neighbourly. It is unkind. There is no sin committed at most of these celebrations. There is no revelry in most of the homes, but simply people trying to honour God the best way they know. When Christians join them courteously it speaks volumes. It is a witness. It shows we care. It shows Jesus cares. It is not compromising our faith. It is not endorsing wrong beliefs. It is reaching out the way Jesus did. We need to learn to be more like Jesus and learn to live with Muslims, to love and draw them to Christ.

To be able to do this we have to first be forgiving. This is where we are unique. We have the one thing that other faiths don't have. In other faiths they love their friends, but they aren't taught to love their enemies. Christians are taught to love all. "Then Jesus said, 'When you give a luncheon or dinner, do not invite your friends, your brothers or sisters, your relatives, or your rich neighbors . . .'" "And if you greet only your own people, what are you doing more than others? Don't even pagans do that? Be perfect, therefore, as your heavenly Father is perfect." We have the one thing that places us in the best position: forgiveness. Use this forgiveness, use this love for enemies Jesus gave us by his Spirit. Use this gift of love, going to these people. We cannot bury our greatest *talent* in Christ. Without it we are no different from others.

How can our societies have peace if their members don't know each other, aren't familiar with each other's families, personal needs and values, don't share joy and pain and everyday activities with each other? How can we have peace if we don't forgive when we are wronged?

Part of our problem is that we haven't drawn close. We have hated multiculturalism and said it has failed. But it can only fail when we fail to actively love, reach and care for each other. We and our churches stay ignorant of cross-cultural skills, but Jesus had these skills in abundance. He challenged the pride of the Syro-Phoenician woman, but healed her daughter. Jews, Greeks, Samaritans and Romans all came to Jesus. Which of them did he refuse? We have the same call. We cannot reject it.

Multiculturalism, when Christ leads the way, enriches our lives. It brings us out of selfishness to overcome the issues that threaten us. Monoculturalism makes us isolated, ignorant and bigoted. Sin brought isolation between God and man and between man and man, but God has now made us to be reconcilers in Christ. Christ is "Reconciler in Chief", showing the way when he pulled down the wall dividing Jew and gentile. (Eph 2:14) We cannot reach the world when we cut ourselves off from people. Considering what Christ did for us, it is sin.

Some of the most technologically advanced cultures in the world are the most relationally deficient when it comes to families and communities. We must turn back to God in this respect. We will gain much if we learn from others. In the past Christianity grew in our separate nation and culture and we were blessed. Today it is growing in a wider and much more challenging context. It is also a more rewarding and holistic context. The whole nature of God is to include others. That's his whole mission in the church. (Eph 1:10) We either go on in the plan of God, sharing his fellowship with all people, or we rot in a swamp cut off from his purpose. (1 John 1:3, Ezek 47:11) As we go forward in God's plan there will be loss and suffering, but also a richer fellowship and a more Christ like community. We only grow in the image of Christ when we learn and grow together. (Eph 4:13) Though the devil has a plan it fails. It is God who is bringing all things together in Christ: what is happening in the world today is God's plan in the gospel.

Community Versus Individualism

In our desire and efforts to retain individual holiness, we can easily forget Jesus' teaching on community values. Since the Reformation the church has practiced protest and separation. Despite many benefits of the Reformation, this separation is not the spirit of Jesus. There are times we have to disagree; times for strong words, but our longsuffering in reaching out should never end. We are far too quick to employ scripture without full understanding, without walking in the shoes of others. We are far too quick to judge and label another. We misinterpret the Apostles' boldness in making declarations to mean that we don't need to speak the Word with love and respect. (Eph 4:15, 1 Pet 2:17, 3:15) We gossip about each other, our brothers and sisters in Christ. We continually separate ourselves into ever increasing numbers of denominations and movements and groups. Our division and separateness, our lack of cooperation, hinders our witness. God, forgive us for doing this in your name!

The scourge of our Western Christian lives is individualism. For as long as we think our faith is just about gaining heaven and shunning the world, we are going to be out of sync with God's plan in this world. When Christianity began to flood the south of Nigeria we realised we must face the north with the gospel. If we didn't care about others, but sought to cut them off, we would be overcome by them. It was a situation of "go to the north with Jesus, or they will come to us with Islam". In the same way we can't cut ourselves off from the world and still hope to keep our society Christian. Christianity never works as something we keep to ourselves and maintain. It is take it to others, or lose it. Meet the world and transform it, or it will transform you. Open up to the world and heal it, or close off to it and be overrun by it.

Our individualism has led us to seek to make the government keep our society Christian as we continue in isolation. Too often we have kept our distance from the sinner and attempted to use the law to achieve God's will in our society, to make laws against the sinner, instead of seeking to serve them. Since the Roman Emperor Constantine converted to the Christian religion we have sought this way out. The early church would not have recognized the church that has often persecuted its enemies and portrayed an entirely different type of "Jesus" to the world.

It's very difficult to be a voice in our society when we have embraced a Christian culture of individualism. How can we rightfully take shots at the sin in our world from the sanctuary of our homes? It seems hypocritical to the unbeliever. "Why don't these Christians live what they preach?" It seems that the only way we can be a light to declining morality is to roll up our sleeves, move out into the dirt and danger of the world and serve others. It is only this abandonment of individualism and self-interest that shows to society the Jesus we see in the Gospels.

We cannot reach across the chasm to Islamic people in our nations with a gospel of individualism. Most Muslims value community. When they come to our nation they need community, but how many Christians are actively seeking to provide it? If newcomers don't find it with us they will find it with others, perhaps even in the message of the Islamic radical. The radical offers more than just a message; it provides an Islamic "umma" (community), giving people something preferable to our individualized, usually selfish and often lonely, separated life style.

So then, what is the answer to the threats we see looming on our horizon, ready to engulf our suburbs and take away our liberties? Our attention has been gained and people are screaming for help. But what is the answer? In the teachings of Jesus there is one answer. It is the kingdom he gave us. When he came the Jews were suffering under an oppressive regime. They expected Jesus to fulfill the prophecies that their King would soon arrive and take away their enemies. They were like us, thinking he would bring in the chariots (army) and make everything right again. They were disappointed, to put it mildly, when they discovered this wasn't the message of Jesus. Jesus' way of dealing with the enemy is radically different.

Instead, Jesus spoke about losing our own life and taking up our own cross. He wasn't just speaking about a way for us to be individually saved, but the way in which his kingdom comes to the world, to our relationships, and the way things are put right in our world today. This is God's goal, to give us his kingdom, this change of heart through faith, to renew this world. This gospel is a long way removed from our individualism. It is good news for our world, not just for us.

Knowing that God's kingdom rule is for this world is one thing; how God does this is another. Jesus said his kingdom is not of this world. That means, it doesn't employ worldly means to succeed. It proceeds through servants. "I came not to be served, but to serve and to give my life as a ransom for many." This atonement statement is also a political statement. Jesus said this to contrast Pilate and other governments like his. (Mark 10:42-45) His atonement is a model for our action in his kingdom on earth. He is commissioning us: "The kingdom of God is within you." It is from within the transformed heart that the world around us is changed.

The statements of Christ "You are the salt of the earth" and "You are the light of the world" are well known to us, but they can easily be taken out of context. (Matt 5:1-16) We think we are above others, "set on a hill" just like Israel did. We think we know what's good and that God means for us to use our power and influence to bring about his will on society. Augustine (AD 354-430) thought like this. The church was to use the state to even "persecute" the heathen, the heretic and the sinner to keep society healthy. The law, government and army have their place, but Christ did not wield these against his enemies. Neither should his church.

Jesus' teaching and model has huge implications for nations. In Nigeria N920 billion ($6.5 billion) was budgeted for the army just to fight the terrorist group Boko Haram. If that was spent on hospitals, education and training in the north, there wouldn't be a Boko Haram. The region would have employment. Likewise, the current terrible human suffering in Syria is not just the fault of the

Syrians. It is because despite the world as a whole's claims of human enlightenment, evolution and advancement, it still acts on the basis of strategic self-interest rather than community. Many Christians still support the former, while the message of Jesus was the latter. These things may not be easily solved, but the church of Jesus should at the very least carry this message.

It was only recently that I realized the significance of the context of Jesus' statements about salt and light. Jesus was speaking about his ways and actions, which were contrary to the way worldly leaders "did" kingdom. He was teaching the crowd 'The Beatitudes', 'The Sermon on the Mount'. His message was his call for us to follow him, to "do" kingdom his way. It was his *modus operandi*, the constitution of the way his kingdom would spread in our world and his rule would extend to all people. It was to be the way of his disciples, what we are to teach others in all nations of the world. Jesus calling us salt and light was in the context of these Beatitudes. It would be through suffering for righteousness, forgiving others, loving our enemies, serving the sinner in going the extra mile, giving our coat as well as our shirt to the one who needs them, seeking peace with others, mourning for the injustice in the world, showing mercy to those in need.

Let's not take this out of context. We are salt and light by doing what Jesus did, by reflecting his image and likeness in the world. As Paul said, "Let this mind be in you that was in Christ Jesus." He gave up his position of power, his comfort zone, and served humanity, even becoming a slave for mankind. So, if we have a hunger for righteousness in our world, if we want our societies to be renewed, then this is to be our call and approach. Serve the Muslim, serve the homosexual, serve the woman who wants an abortion, converting others to the true Son of God, and saving our own nation from false Christianity expressed in self-centred individualism.

The Real Kingdom of God

Jesus' way was to strike at the sin that's within our hearts and fill the earth with a community of people who followed his way of life. He knew the Holy Spirit would transform our hearts because of his cross, compelling us into a call to serve and love each other. This community is the stone that becomes the mountain filling the earth while Christ rules at Father's right hand. (Dan 2:35, 7:13-14)

The Jews had heard of a Messiah who would suffer and then ascend to heaven to rule all nations. They asked who these people were who would rule with him. The Jewish leaders answered: those who keep Torah. Paul answered: those who are of faith that works through love. Jesus answered: those who serve, for this is Torah and faith.

Just as some Replacement Theologians said God was judging the Jews in European history, today some Dispensationalists say God is judging the Arabs and Palestinians, even the Christians among them, for the sake of the nation of Israel. These two theologies have the same result; they are just the same shoes on two different feet. Both miss the point. The church Jesus called, by total contrast, is like the Good Samaritan who reaches out to serve the suffering whoever they are. The church is no respecter of persons, no judge of unbelievers. We are called to serve, to help, to rescue, to give, not to judge. God will judge all at the end.

Jesus announced a kingdom, his community, creating a new world through his resurrection power. A community that treats each member as if he or she were Jesus himself, shines the light of the gospel on conservatism, liberalism, individualism, violence, terrorism, greed, immorality, nationalism, tribalism and the corruption of a decaying society. That is how God renews the world: through his people being a witness (which also means martyr), not by force. This is what the Bible calls the "foolishness of God", and it is wiser than man. This is the wisdom the church reveals to a sinful world. (Eph 3:10)

When the disciple asked Jesus to teach them to pray, Jesus answered by revealing a community. The first word of the Lord's prayer is "Our". The second word "Father" means we have family whom we are called to love. This is how "Your kingdom come and your will be done on earth as it is in heaven" works. When Jesus launched his kingdom on the cross he said to John, "Behold your mother", and to Mary, "Behold your son". From that point on we are to treat each one as our own flesh and blood.

The New Testament points us to relationships: Jesus saying "Take the log out of your own eye", James saying "Confess your faults and pray for each other that you may be healed" in your relationships, Paul saying "Restore the one who has fallen." "Forgive and love your enemy." "When you have wronged your neighbor, go and make it right". We are to take these steps before we expect others to, before we actively seek justice for others locally and globally. These are the things Jesus meant when he said, "If you call me Lord, why don't you do the things I say?" This skill or "technology" in relationships is a solution our cultures desperately need. Our marriages, children, neighbours, churches, communities and community of nations need this more than anything else.

In Christ's kingdom our churches are not cultural enclaves. We look for the weak, those struggling with sin, those of foreign cultures, or from other faiths. This is the nature of Christ, always seeking to include, where fellowship isn't complete until we find every lost sheep, along with our family from all Christian traditions. The Muslim finds true "umma" in the kingdom, discovering it doesn't happen by

Sharia law, but by the Spirit. We don't shun sinners, but call them in to learn with us how to die to self together. Repentance is for us all, until we are conformed together to the full image of Christ. We can't reach the Muslim or the sinner without an ongoing simplicity and repentance in us that brings about true Christ-like community to nourish all in need.

This is the "one-another" focus we find in all of Paul's letters: members one of another, pray for one another, love one another, forgive one another, submit to one another, care for one another, bear with one another, be kind and compassionate with one-another, condescend to one another, carry one another's burdens, build up one another, consider one another better than yourself, be devoted to one another, live in harmony with one another. We have focused in Paul's epistles on our individual position in Christ, while this isn't Paul's focus at all. His focus is that we all of different backgrounds and traditions have one justification in Christ by faith, resulting in us being grafted into one household. It's this community in the world, the fulfillment of the promise to Abraham, which Paul is declaring with a trumpet. This community in Christ is the Good News, the community in Acts, sharing everything they had with each other.

We are called to turn away from the symbols of the Greek gods: our houses, cars, careers, credit cards . . . which in part have built our societies. The Greek gods are lust, violence, power, wealth, ego, competition, divisions, private lives, control of others. God calls us to reflect his image, the Trinity in love fellowship, to the world through community. We may live in houses and use cars, but we reject these as symbols of our individualism, and instead enhance the symbols of family which seeks to embrace all other people in care. The symbols of God's community are the manger, the donkey, the bread, the wine, the cross, the empty tomb, the tongues of fire . . . by which we are given to reach the poor, bring peace to the world, and to nourish each other through the Holy Spirit, as Christ was given for us and now lives in us by faith. This is the power of God bringing healing to us and our world.

I wonder how I can have missed this part of the gospel for so long: His name shall be called the Prince of Peace; of the increase of his government and peace (in this age) there shall be no end; none shall hurt or harm on all his holy mountain; they (as a result of the gospel) shall beat their swords into ploughs; the wolf and lamb shall lie down together; the fruit of justice shall be peace; you, David, shall not build my house for you have been a man of war but I will raise up your seed and he will be a man of peace and he will build my (global) kingdom; the Spirit came on Jesus in the form of a dove; peace on earth and good will to all men; blessed are the peacemakers; take the log out of your own eye; forgive and love your enemy; put things right with those you have wronged; take up your cross and follow me; he rode into Jerusalem on a donkey (a symbol showing his is a kingdom of peace) and said "If only you had known the ways of peace"; our shoes are shod with the gospel of peace; overcome evil with good. This is Christ's people-centred community.

Just as Christ rose from the dead and sits today at the place of authority over the entire world, so God's power and kingdom shall proceed through all nations and people, until the meek (not the oppressor) inherit the earth. Let's make sure we reflect this kingdom to all in our societies and in our community of nations.

His Glory Will
Cover the World

Just weeks ago I was in Jos, getting into the car early one morning to head to the Bible College office. That morning I put on the radio and tuned in to a local station. The entire way to the office I listened to the most beautiful worship music. It brought my heart to tears. Things could have been so different, before our sudden miracle. We didn't deserve this. God has been so good. You can imagine our gratitude and joy! Emanuel Razack, co-founder of the ministry in Jos with Ruth and me, had called this year 2013 *"The Year of Unusual Miracles"*, and so it has proven to be. Before the miracle, I had been accustomed to heading down the same road through suburbs deserted because of the conflict, past vehicles at the military check points, tanks and troop carriers, and under helicopter gunships overhead. Now, there was peace.

The peaceful contrast sparked emotions as I thought about the Christians of Jos. They had refused to be intimidated, refused to give up their faith in Jesus Christ. Islamic terrorists had demanded they leave their churches and their faith or die, and many did die, but they had refused to give up. Once again God brought them through, and the first thing they did was fill the city with worship music on secular radio to share their joy and love. If I had a hundred hats I would take them all off to the believers of northern Nigeria! They won against Satan's last card, the fear of death. Now, so many Muslims are coming to Christ. This region is being transformed by the gospel. The fight of faith continues for many. Many still give their lives for their faith. Newly born believers are nurtured, protected and supported by local Christians, loving those who formerly tried to kill them.

Our experiences show that we overcome by loving our enemies and by loving those in need: "I was hungry and you fed me, in prison and sick and you visited me." When we do this for any person, even those of another faith, we are doing it for Jesus. In Australia we know people who help boat arrivals, refugees and other immigrants. They love them and help them settle into community and many also become baptized believers. Other Australians help them in their immigration prisons or refugee camps on nearby islands. These and so many other refugees around the world desperately need Jesus' love from Jesus' people.

Miracles happen as we go out to share the love of Jesus with others. Stories abound of God touching lives, giving visions, healing bodies, opening doors, changing the hearts of rulers, reworking circumstances, giving mountain-moving faith, providing for needs, changing communities, bringing great revival. The biggest worldwide miracles the church has ever seen will happen in the next 100 years. 500 years ago they said its over for the church due to Islam, yet these have been the church's most expansive years. 100 years ago they said its over for the church in Africa, yet it was Africa's best century for evangelism. The "experts" will once again be shocked in the next 100 years as God brings in the greatest worldwide harvest and growth of his church in all nations. "I will build my church and the gates of hell will not prevail against it—will not prevent its triumphant progress." "I will give you the nations for your inheritance, the ends of the earth for your possession."

The email below from a pastor and friend in Australia is a good way to close this booklet:

"My husband and I have been seated listening to your recent message. I was still in Kenya when you visited our church, so it was good to be able to hear your message. I have been reading your book, ~~Changing the World~~, *Changing Ourselves* since I got home, and we were both very moved, enlightened and challenged as we listened again to your message together. We want to make copies of the message and send them to our Leaders/Sons in the Lord in Uganda, Kenya and South Sudan.

I had been led by the Lord to the scriptures where Jesus talked about if we only love those who love us how are we better than pagans who also do this, but that we are to actively love our enemies in word and deed and attitude!! This was in a church in Luwero, in Uganda, and the Spirit of God truly ignited the message to the congregation there. Praise God!

I have truly felt so exercised about reaching out to Muslims within our local areas in Australia. There are so many living here, but most Christians avoid them like the plague! In the 'too hard basket' as it were. I am seeking God as to how this can be overcome and for ways to engage with these Muslim people, rather than fear them, and sending scaremongering emails around to all our 'Christian' friends, as some do!! I have such a desire to go door to door or somehow be able to engage people in open discussion about the things of God and His love for the world."

"Lift up your heads, you gates; lift them up, you ancient doors so that the King of glory may come in." (Psalm 24:9)

Christ ascended to heaven, and his blood has also opened all gates on earth. It has opened the gates of the temple to let his presence out to the nations. (Ezek 47) It has opened the gates of Satan: the nations, borders, camps and ideologies set up against Christ's church, to let God's power and glory flood through to people's souls. Christ commissioned the church to go through open doors when he said, "I saw Satan fall . . ." Let's open our doors and let the King of glory flood through to all nations, to all people of all faiths. It's time for open hearts, open doors, open churches and open houses, for a great harvest, for his promises among all nations to be fulfilled. His glory will cover the world!!

Would You Like To

- Obtain more copies or bundles of *Crossing the Chasm* to share with others
- Obtain copies of the book *Fearless Love*, miracles and conversions among Muslims of Jos
- Obtain copies of ~~Changing the World~~, *Changing Ourselves*, the global apocalypse and the Sermon on the Mount
- Invite Kent & Ruth to speak
- Support the mission

Email: kent.hodge@cfaithministries.org,
go to cfaithministries.org, or see details below . . .

In Australia

Acc. Name: Christian Faith Ministries Int.

Westpac, BSB: 032870 Acc. No: 207255

In the UK

Acc. Name: Christian Faith Ministries Int.

Sort Code: 401322 Acc. No: 61775723

Charity registration number: 1137723

All gifts are used 100% to support the spread of the gospel through evangelism, pastoral training, interior grass-roots missions and rural education, convert care and discipleship, children's schooling and care, and vocational education for community development. Kent & Ruth do not draw a wage from the ministry nor are funds to these accounts used to support Kent & Ruth.

+ 12244001573